New EXPLORE History

TUDOR WORLD

HAYDN MIDDLETON

Heinemann

www.heinemann.co.uk/library
Visit our website to find out more information about **Heinemann Library** books.

To order:
- ☎ Phone 44 (0) 1865 888066
- 🖹 Send a fax to 44 (0) 1865 314091
- 🖥 Visit the Heinemann Bookshop at www.heinemann.co.uk/library to browse our catalogue and order online.

First published in Great Britain by Heinemann Library, Halley Court, Jordan Hill, Oxford OX2 8EJ, part of Harcourt Education. Heinemann is a registered trademark of Harcourt Education Ltd.

Editorial: Jilly Attwood, Kathy Peltan and Vicki Yates
Design: Dave Poole and Tokay Interactive Ltd
Picture Research: Hannah Taylor
Production: Camilla Smith

Originated by Chroma Graphics (Overseas) Pte. Ltd
Printed in China by WKT Company Limited

ISBN 0 431 07904 8 (hardback)
10 09 08 07 06
10 9 8 7 6 5 4 3 2 1

ISBN 0 431 07910 2 (paperback)
10 09 08 07 06
10 9 8 7 6 5 4 3 2 1

British Library Cataloguing in Publication Data
Middleton, Haydn
Tudor World
942'.05
A full catalogue record for this book is available from the British Library.

Acknowledgements
The publishers would like to thank the following for permission to reproduce photographs:
AKG Images p. **26**; Alamy Images p. **11** (Justin Kase); Bridgeman Art Library p. **8** (Victoria & Albert Museum), **19, 25, 32, 40, 41**(Private Collection), **36** (Kunsthistorisches Museum), pp. **18, 24**; Corbis pp. **14** (Bettmann), **34** (Archivo Iconografico, S.A.); Getty Images p. **43**, p. **9t** (Image Source); Harcourt Education Ltd pp. **20, 23** (Trevor Clifford), **21** (Phil Bratt), **27** (Tudor Photography), **28** (Peter Evans), **35** (Debbie Rowe); Historic Royal Palaces p. **9b**; Museum of London p. **29** (Horners Co); (National Maritime Museum pp. **30, 31, 33, 38, 42**; National Portrait Gallery pp. **4, 6, 10, 12, 16, 17**; Royal Collection p. **13**; Topham Picturepoint p. **15** (Fotomas).

...roduced ...Gallery.

...n for ...book.

...yright ...book. ...ent printings if notice is given to the publishers.

Any words appearing in the text in bold, **like this**, are explained in the glossary.

Contents

Exploring further

Throughout the book you will find links to the Heinemann Explore CD-ROM and website at www.heinemannexplore.co.uk Follow the links to discover more about a topic.

What do the symbols mean?

The following symbols are used throughout the book:

Source

See for yourself

Biography

How many times did Henry VIII marry?

Kings and queens in Tudor times did not marry for love. They married into other rich and powerful families, often from other countries. Henry VIII married six times. He had three children: Edward, Mary, and Elizabeth.

The Tudors

Henry VIII was a member of the Tudor royal family. They ruled Britain from 1485 to 1603. The first Tudor king was Henry VII. Henry VIII was his son. Henry VIII's children were also Tudor **monarchs**.

The most married king

Henry VIII ruled England from 1509 to 1547. When he married, he wanted to have a son, a male **heir** who would take over from him as king when he died. His first marriage was to Katharine of Aragon in 1509. She was a princess from Spain. She gave birth to a daughter, Mary, in 1516, but she never gave Henry a son that lived. He divorced Katharine and married Anne Boleyn in 1533. She had a daughter called Elizabeth. Henry fell out with Anne, and in 1536 he had her **beheaded**.

This portrait of Henry VIII was painted in 1536, the year he married Jane Seymour. He was 44 years old. It was painted by Hans Holbein, a famous artist at Henry's **court**. The rich clothes and jewels make the king look powerful.

Just eleven days after Anne's death, Henry married Jane Seymour. She, at last, gave Henry the son he wanted, Edward. However, Jane died soon after the baby was born. Next, Henry married Anne of Cleves. She was the sister of a powerful German prince, but Henry did not like Anne and divorced her after only six months. By this time Henry was 49 years old.

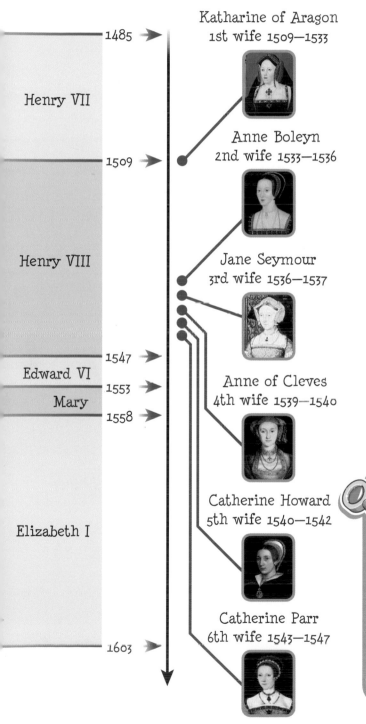

Henry VII

1485

Katharine of Aragon
1st wife 1509—1533

1509

Anne Boleyn
2nd wife 1533—1536

Henry VIII

Jane Seymour
3rd wife 1536—1537

1547

Edward VI

1553

Mary

1558

Anne of Cleves
4th wife 1539—1540

Elizabeth I

Catherine Howard
5th wife 1540—1542

1603

Catherine Parr
6th wife 1543—1547

Henry's next wife was Catherine Howard. She was very young, and their marriage did not last long. She was beheaded in 1542 when Henry found out she had been seeing other men. Henry's last wife was Catherine Parr. He married her in 1543. She was still his wife when he died in 1547.

No English king has ever been married as many times as Henry VIII. This rhyme may help you to remember what happened to his six wives: 'Divorced, beheaded, died. Divorced, beheaded, survived.'

Exploring further

The Heinemann Explore website and CD-ROM includes text on all the key topics about the Tudors. You will also find pictures, biographies, written sources, and lots of activities to explore. Start at the Contents screen. Click on the blue words in the list and off you go!

What was Henry VIII like as a person?

It can be hard to find out what people from long ago were really like. However, we can look at pictures of them, and read descriptions written by people who knew them and then try to decide for ourselves.

This portrait of Henry was painted in 1520, when he was about 30 years old. He looks much younger than in the portrait on page 4.

Portraits as evidence

Many portraits were painted of Henry VIII. They are useful evidence. They show us how Henry wanted to be seen. They also show us how he changed as he got older. As a young man, Henry was tall, strong, and good-looking. As he grew older, he became fatter and much less fit.

This description of Henry VIII was written by an Italian in England in 1515, when the king was about 24 years old.

*His Majesty is the handsomest ruler I have ever set eyes on; above the usual height, with an extremely fine calf to his leg, his complexion very fair and bright, with auburn hair combed short and straight ... He speaks French, English, and Latin, and a little Italian, plays well on the **lute** and **harpsichord**, sings from book at sight, draws the bow with greater strength than any man in England, and **jousts** marvellously ... he is in every respect a most accomplished prince.*

A hero

Henry worked hard at being a good king. He wanted his people to think of him as a hero. One of his **courtiers**, Lord Mountjoy, said, 'Our king does not desire gold or gems or precious metals, but virtue [and] glory.'

A scholar king

Henry also enjoyed talking to people he found interesting, such as **scholars**. One of these, Thomas More, said that Henry liked to discuss many subjects with him, including mathematics and 'the courses of the stars and planets'. Henry also liked to relax with music, **real tennis** and hunting.

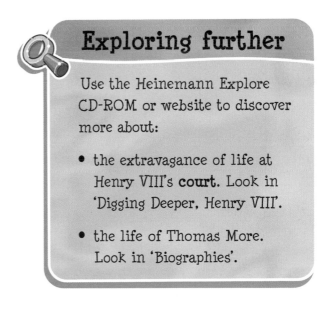

Exploring further

Use the Heinemann Explore CD-ROM or website to discover more about:

- the extravagance of life at Henry VIII's **court**. Look in 'Digging Deeper, Henry VIII'.

- the life of Thomas More. Look in 'Biographies'.

What did Henry VIII do all day?

From 1509 to 1547, Henry VIII was the most important person in England. He had servants and **courtiers** to make his life comfortable, and advisers to help him **govern** the country.

Governing the kingdom

Today, the **government** runs the country. In Henry VIII's time, things were different. Henry was very powerful. He had to make sure all his people and his noblemen obeyed him and the laws. He also had to make sure that everybody paid their taxes, to raise the money for the things he wanted to do.

Wars

Henry VIII wanted to win glory for England and for himself in war. He went to war often with England's old enemy, France, and with Scotland. Some wars he won, some he lost, but he did not get much for England out of the wars.

This writing box was made for Henry VIII in the 1520s. It is lined with leather, which is painted with the royal **coat of arms** and with the Roman gods Mars, Venus, and Cupid. Henry would have used the opened box to write on when he was working.

Thomas Wolsey

Cardinal Wolsey (1475–1530) was the son of a butcher from Ipswich in Suffolk. He became a bishop, then a **cardinal**. In 1515 he became Lord Chancellor, the king's most powerful Minister. He helped the king to govern the country. He became very rich. He fell from power in 1529, when he failed to persuade the Pope to allow Henry to divorce Katharine of Aragon.

See for yourself

Hampton Court Palace, London

Hampton Court Palace, on the bank of the River Thames west of London, was a royal palace in Henry VIII's time. Here, Henry and his **court** conducted their business and lived in great style. The palace had belonged to Cardinal Wolsey, but it passed to Henry before Wolsey fell from power. Henry turned it into one of the most modern, sophisticated, and magnificent palaces in England. There were **real tennis** courts, bowling alleys and pleasure gardens, a hunting park, a jousting yard, huge kitchens, a chapel, a great hall for dining, and a multiple garderobe, or lavatory, which could sit 28 people at a time.

Henry held lavish entertainments at Hampton Court, often for important foreign visitors. Many staff were needed to run the palace. The kitchens and wine cellars alone had over 350 servants.

Why did Henry VIII divorce Katharine of Aragon?

In Tudor times, not many people got a divorce. If a king, like Henry VIII, wanted a divorce, he had to ask the Pope in Rome. The Pope was head of the **Catholic** Church. At that time, England was a Catholic country. However, when Henry asked for a divorce from Queen Katharine of Aragon, the Pope said no.

The need for a son and heir

Henry desperately wanted a son to be his **heir**. He thought that when he died, only a strong son could carry on ruling the country. His first wife Katharine of Aragon had four sons, but they all died as babies. In 1531, Henry ignored the Pope and left Katharine.

The Reformation

Henry's break with Rome was part of a much bigger religious change in Europe. This was called the **Reformation** because it tried to reform, or change, the Catholic Church. When this failed, new **Protestant** ('protesting') churches were founded. Protestants wanted churches to be well organized, and worshipping to be simpler. Henry was not a Protestant. He believed in the Catholic ways of worship, but he would not obey the Pope.

Katharine of Aragon was the daughter of King Ferdinand and Queen Isabella of Spain. She had been married to Henry's older brother, Arthur, before he died.

A new Church of England

Henry had to set up a new Church of England. He then made himself its leader. In 1533, Henry was given his divorce by an archbishop in his new Church, called Thomas Cranmer. Henry's divorce changed England for ever. England now had its own Church and was not part of the Catholic Church. This meant that Henry had an **alliance** with the Protestants.

Tintern Abbey was closed down by Cromwell's men in 1536. Its ruins remain today. Some monastery churches were saved. Smaller ones became local parish churches. Larger ones became cathedrals, for example at Peterborough and St Albans. Some monasteries even became houses for the rich.

The end of the monasteries

At the time Henry became head of the English Church, priests were unpopular with both nobles and peasants. They thought priests were rich, greedy, and lazy. Henry decided to reform the Church and take its wealth for himself. In 1536 and 1539,

Exploring further

Use the Heinemann Explore CD-ROM or website to find out more about the Reformation in England. Look in 'Digging Deeper, Henry VIII, The break with Rome'.

Parliament passed laws dissolving, or getting rid of, the **monasteries**. Cromwell's men visited over 800 abbeys, monasteries, and other religious houses. They sent the priests away, seized the money and other treasures, and destroyed the buildings. This made the king very rich.

Thomas Cromwell

Thomas Cromwell (1485–1540) was Henry VIII's chief **minister** from 1534 to 1540. He was clever and worked hard. Cromwell was a Protestant. He helped to start the English Reformation, closing down the monasteries. Cromwell had many enemies among the king's **courtiers**. In 1540, they told Henry that Cromwell was not to be trusted. Henry had just made Cromwell the Earl of Essex, but he believed the rumours. Henry had Cromwell executed without a trial.

Did marrying Anne Boleyn or Jane Seymour solve Henry's problems?

In the late 1520s, Henry VIII began looking for a new wife. He still needed a son. Henry fell for a young Englishwoman called Anne Boleyn.

Anne Boleyn

Anne came from a noble family. In January 1533, Henry and Anne were married in secret. Anne was made queen just before she gave birth to Henry's child. However, the child was not a boy, it was a girl, Elizabeth.

Anne was not liked in Henry's **court**. His friends told him many bad tales about her. Some even said she had been seeing other men. When she did not have a son, Henry became impatient with her and more likely to believe the bad tales. Finally, in 1536, Henry had Anne **beheaded** in the Tower of London.

Anne Boleyn was lively, well educated, and twenty years younger than Henry's first wife, Katharine. However, she did not give Henry the son he longed for.

Jane Seymour

Henry was already in love with another young woman, called Jane Seymour. He married her only eleven days after Anne died. On 12 October 1537, Jane gave Henry what he most wanted – a son. The boy was named Edward. Sadly, Jane herself died only twelve days later. Henry was heartbroken.

Would Henry marry again?

Henry now had a son and **heir**. However in Tudor times, one son was not enough. Many children died when they were young. Henry needed another son in case Edward died.

There was another reason why Henry needed a new wife. His argument with the Pope had left England with many powerful enemies abroad. If Henry married a **Protestant** princess, he would have an **alliance** with another protestant country. This would help Henry if he needed to fight his enemies.

Jane Seymour was quiet and modest, unlike Anne Boleyn. She had been Anne's **lady-in-waiting**. She is painted here with Henry and their longed-for son, Edward, although in fact she died when Edward was only twelve days old.

Exploring further

Use the Heinemann Explore website or CD-ROM to find out more about:

- Henry's marriage to Anne Boleyn, in the Activity 'Henry VIII and Anne Boleyn'.

- the new union between England and Wales when the baby Edward was made Prince of Wales. Look in 'Digging Deeper, Henry VIII, Birth of an heir'.

- Jane Seymour's brother, Edward Seymour, who was to become an important adviser to Edward VI. Look in 'Biographies'.

Why did Henry's marriage to Anne of Cleves fail?

Henry VIII married Anne of Cleves for political reasons, not for love. When he met her, it was obvious the marriage would not last.

Making friends in Europe

The **Catholic** rulers of France and Spain did not like what Henry had done to the Church of England. He was afraid they were going to invade England. Henry needed to make friends with other **Protestant** rulers who were not friendly with the rulers of France and Spain. Duke William of Cleves was a prince from Germany, another Protestant country. He had a young sister called Anne. By marrying Anne, Henry could ask the duke to help him fight in any wars with France and Spain. Thomas Cromwell arranged the marriage.

Henry goes ahead

Anne came to England in December 1539. Henry had never seen her before. When they met, he thought she was very ugly, but he still needed to marry her. On 6 January 1540, Henry married for the fourth time.

The talented **court** artist Hans Holbein was sent to Germany to paint Anne's portrait, so that Henry could see what she looked like. This is that portrait. Holbein made her look more attractive than she really was, so that Henry would like her.

This Protestant picture dates from 1545. It shows the Pope with a monster that represents the Catholic Church. This was a time of bitter religious arguments.

A disaster

The marriage to Anne of Cleves was a disaster. The Catholic kings did not invade England, so Henry did not have to stay married to her. Before the end of 1540, Henry and Anne were divorced. Henry blamed Cromwell for the marriage, and he did not trust him any more. Cromwell was accused of treason, **condemmned** and **beheaded** in June 1540.

Henry gave Anne two houses and £500 per year to live on. Anne stayed in England until she died in 1557.

Exploring further

Use the Heinemann Explore CD-ROM, or go to the website to find out more about the **Reformation** in Europe. Look in 'Biographies, Martin Luther'.

Why did Henry marry Catherine Howard and Catherine Parr?

Henry gave up the idea of making an **alliance** by marriage in Europe, but he still wanted more sons. Soon after divorcing Anne of Cleves, he married a pretty **courtier** called Catherine Howard.

Catherine Howard

Catherine was only twenty years old when she married Henry VIII in 1540. Henry was 50. Catherine came from a powerful **Catholic** family, so the marriage pleased the Catholics in Britain and abroad. However, Henry believed that Catherine was having relationships with other men, which made him furious. Early in 1542 she was **beheaded**.

This portrait of Catherine Howard was also painted by the court painter, Hans Holbein.

Catherine Parr

Henry married his last wife, Catherine Parr, in July 1543. She was a 36-year-old **Protestant** woman from his **court**. She was clever, quiet, and sensible, and she looked after the king as he grew more ill. When Henry died in 1547, Catherine married again and had a daughter.

Catherine Parr and Henry never had any children, but she was a loving mother to Henry's children, Mary, Elizabeth, and Edward.

Why did Henry VIII marry six times?

Henry's main concern was to make sure that the **Tudors** would keep ruling England after he died. He lived in a time when the **monarch** had to control powerful families to keep a grip on power. Marriage helped Henry to build alliances with foreign rulers and with powerful courtiers.

Henry believed that only a boy could inherit his kingdom. However, after he died, his son Edward ruled for only six years before he also died, in 1553. Henry's elder daughter, Mary, became

Exploring further

Use the Heinemann Explore CD-ROM or website to find out more about:

- a painting of Henry VIII on his deathbed, pointing to his son Edward who was to succeed him. Look in 'Pictures, Invasion and Warfare'.

- the difference between Catholic and Protestant beliefs in the Activity 'Catholics and Protestants'.

queen. She also ruled for five years (1553–1558). When she died, Henry's daughter Elizabeth became queen. Elizabeth I ruled for 45 years (1558–1603). Many think she was a better ruler than her father. Elizabeth said, 'I know I have the body of a weak and feeble woman, but I have the heart and stomach of a king. And a king of England too.'

What was different about rich and poor people in Tudor times?

The lives of rich people were very different from the lives of poor people in Tudor times. There are many kinds of evidence we can use to find out about them.

The writings of people who lived in Tudor times are a good source of evidence. In 1577, a clergyman called William Harrison wrote a *Description of England*. This is how he divided up the English people:

We in England divide our people into four sorts. First there are the gentlemen: after the king, the chief gentlemen are the princes, dukes, marquises, earls, viscounts, and barons. After them are knights, esquires, and last of all they that are simply called gentlemen.
*Second to the gentlemen come the **citizens**. They live in the cities, and probably do important jobs there.*
Third come the yeomen. They are freeborn Englishmen and own a certain amount of land. [These men were often rich farmers, just below the gentlemen.]
*The fourth and last sort of people in England are day labourers, poor husbandmen [farmworkers], some **retailers** who have no free land... and all craftsmen such as tailors, shoemakers, carpenters, bricklayers, masons, etc.*

Paintings are another valuable kind of evidence. This picture of Lord Cobham and his family was painted in 1567. Their expensive clothes, pets, and the food on the table all show that this was a wealthy family. The five year-old twin girls and their four-year-old sister are dressed like miniature adults. The eldest son, William, sits in front of his father.

Rich and poor

There were not many rich people in Tudor times, but those who were rich lived in great comfort. They paid servants and workers to look after their large homes and lands.

The poor had hardly anything of their own. Most Tudor people lived in villages. They worked for the owner of the land around the village. They rented patches of ground from him to grow their crops. Their few cows, pigs, and poultry grazed on common land. In good years, they could feed themselves and have food left over to sell at market. In bad years, they went hungry.

Not enough jobs

In the Tudor period, the number of people in England increased, but the number of jobs did not. Things also cost more, but wages stayed the same. All this meant that there were a lot of people without jobs who were very poor. Some even had to beg and steal to stay alive.

Working on farms was hard, but all the family helped out. The men and boys did the heavy work. The women and girls made cheese, butter, bread, and beer, looked after the cattle, and took fruit to market.

How comfortable were the lives of rich Tudor people?

Before Tudor times, the homes of very rich people were more like castles than homes. After about 1500, this started to change. Rich people began to build houses that were more comfortable to live in. When Henry VIII closed down the **monasteries** in 1536, he sold many of them to rich people. They turned them into grand houses for themselves.

New trends

Big houses were made of timber, plaster, stone, and brick. They also had many glass windows. Early Tudor houses had no upstairs. They had very high ceilings, with a hole in the roof for smoke from a fire to go through. People sat round the fire in a big hall. They did not have their own rooms. This all changed when chimneys started being built in the new houses. Later Tudor houses had many smaller rooms, instead of one large hall. Each room had its own fireplace.

This is the **parlour** of the house in Stratford-upon-Avon where William Shakespeare was born and grew up. The family cooked and ate in a separate dining room.

Home comforts

Rich people's houses had new home comforts: oak chairs and tables, paintings and **tapestries** on the walls, and four-poster beds with curtains to pull round at night. There were fine wood carvings on staircases, doors, and panels. The ceilings, too, were decorated with plaster patterns. Yet they had no running water, no bathroom, no indoor toilet, a few soft chairs, and no carpets. What was thought comfortable in Tudor times would not seem so comfortable today.

The grandest houses

Among the great houses of the time were Hampton Court, built between 1514 and 1536 and Hardwick Hall built in 1597, for Bess of Hardwick. These homes were far grander than any in Britain since Roman times, with their many windows and tall chimneys. Many large houses were built in the **half-timbered** style, but by the early 17th century stone was thought more suitable for a country mansion.

See for yourself

Bramall Hall, Stockport

Bramall Hall is a magnificent example of a black-and-white, timber-framed manor house. The walls are plastered between the timbers. The house was built in the 15th century and was enlarged both in the 1590s and in 1609. The house was the home of the Davenports, an important local family, for several hundred years. Inside, the house was changed a lot in Victorian times, but it is still possible to see grand Tudor plaster ceilings and paintings.

What can inventories tell us about the lives of people at this time?

In early Tudor times, when someone died, a list was made of everything they owned. This list was called an **inventory**. Poor people's inventories were not very long. Some may have only had a table, a bench, and a few sacks of straw to sleep on. Some poor families lived with their pigs and cows. Their homes were made of wood and had no glass in the windows.

Homes of the rich

A rich person's inventory would be much longer. Rich people had many things in their houses to make them look beautiful. Their best room was the **parlour**. It might have carved wood on the walls, plaster patterns on the ceilings, and colourful glass windows.

This is part of a gentleman's inventory. John Lawson lived in Chester in Cheshire. He was quite a rich man. The inventory listed his things and what they would cost to buy. The prices are in old money (s means shilling, d means pence). These are some of the things on his list:

In the hall:

One iron fireplace, with all the parts belonging to it, 6s 8d.

One table, 1 carpet, 1 bench, 2 chairs with a little chair and 1 box for salt, 13s 4d.

One cupboard with a chest and a pair of tables, 18s.

Eleven cushions, 4s.

One dagger with a hanger, 5s.

In the parlour:

One standing bed with 1 feather bed, 1 pair of woollen blankets, 2 coverlets, 1 covering, 1 bolster, 1 pillow, with woollen hangings, 22s.

A more comfortable life

William Harrison wrote in his *Description of England* in 1577 that homes now had more furniture than in the past. Even workmen and farmers 'have learned to decorate ... their well-made beds with **tapestry** and silk hangings, and their tables with carpets and fine cloth.'

The **wills** left by dead people show us that Harrison was right. By the end of the Tudor period, more ordinary people were using beds, and maybe they had a chest or two to store things in. They were also starting to use 'proper' tables and chairs, rather than folding tables and benches.

This bedroom in the Shakespeares' house is thought to be where William Shakespeare was born. Woollen hangings surround the bed, and painted cloths hang on the walls.

William Shakespeare

William Shakespeare (1564–1616) was a brilliant English playwright and poet. He is still probably the world's most famous writer. He was born in Stratford-upon-Avon in Warwickshire. In 1582, he married Anne Hathaway and they had three children. Shakespeare travelled to London to work as an actor and writer of plays. His band of actors often performed at **court**. From 1599 to 1613 they acted at the Globe Theatre in London.

Shakespeare died in 1616 and was buried at Stratford-upon-Avon. Most of his plays are still performed today. They include comedies such as *A Midsummer Night's Dream* and *As You Like It*, and tragedies such as *Hamlet* and *Macbeth*. Shakespeare also wrote many poems.

What was life like for poor people in Tudor times?

There were a lot of poor people in Tudor times. Some of them had jobs, but still could not earn enough to look after their families. Others were too ill or disabled to work. Some could not find jobs, and others, called **vagrants**, lived by going around begging or stealing from others.

The deserving poor

The very old, sick, widows, and children without parents were called the deserving poor. They could not work, so their families, friends, and local church helped them.

In this painting by a Dutch painter called Pieter Brueghel, bread is being given to the deserving poor. Rich people often left money in their **wills** to be spent on giving food to the poor on a particular day each year.

Children

Children from poor families had to work or beg. In the towns, they lived with many other families in **slum** buildings. In the country, they lived in one-roomed cottages or sheds. The very poorest had to sleep on the streets or under hedges.

Vagrants were often whipped in the streets in Tudor times.

Vagrants

Vagrants moved around the country looking for work, begging, or stealing. Other people, such as travelling actors, were often thought of as vagrants, but they did not usually cause trouble.

A growing problem

As England's population rose, there were fewer jobs. Many people were out of work. Peasants were forced from their villages by landlords who fenced off their fields and common lands to make grazing land for their own sheep. By 1570, there were more than 10,000 homeless people wandering the roads, looking for work and begging.

The Fulborne family

Alexander Fulborne and his wife Agnes lived in Norwich. They were both aged 40 in 1570. Alexander had trained as a tailor, but could not find work. Agnes knitted to make money. Their daughters, aged seventeen and twelve, spun wool. They were given **alms** of 2d (2 pence) per week, and were described as 'very poor' in the records.

Exploring further

Use the Heinemann Explore CD-ROM or visit the website to find out more about:

- the lives of Tudor children. Look in 'Digging Deeper, Tudor children'.

- Tudor towns, trade and transport. Look in 'Digging Deeper'.

The government takes action

Before Tudor times, the **government** gave no help to the poor. The Tudor **Parliament** passed **Poor Laws** to try to help them. The first laws were very hard on poor people, because the rulers thought they were just being lazy. Some laws said that disabled beggars were to be whipped and sent home if they moved outside their local area.

By 1603, the laws were more helpful. The old, sick, widowed, and orphaned had to be looked after by people living in their villages or towns. Work also had to be found for the fit.

This painting shows a travelling **pedlar**, who went round the countryside selling cheap goods. New laws made it harder for poor people to travel around, even to look for work when times were hard. This was because the government was afraid they might group together and cause trouble.

Thomas Harman was a **Justice of the Peace** in 1567. His views about vagrants were shared by many people.

I thought it my duty to tell you of the wicked and detestable behaviour of all these ragged rabble who – under the pretence of great misery, disease, or disaster – manage to gain alms from good people in all places.

Almshouses

One of the ways in which local people could help the poor was by providing **alms**houses. These were built to house the deserving poor. Rich people gave money for them to be built and repaired. They left instructions for this in their **wills**, many of which have survived. You can still see Tudor almshouses in many towns today.

These Tudor almshouses are in Ewelme, Oxfordshire.

Humphrey Gibbons

Humphrey Gibbons was arrested as a **vagrant** in New Romney, Kent, in 1596. He said that in 1586 he had owned a large farm. He had been forced to sell it because of rising prices and bad harvests. He worked as a labourer for three years, until he could afford to buy another small farm. In 1596 the harvest failed, and he was forced to become a travelling labourer again.

How different were the lives of rich and poor people?

The lives of all Tudor people, both rich and poor, were very different from our lives today. However, the differences between the lives of the rich and the poor were also enormous in Tudor times.

The Tudor view of the world

Tudor people had different views about life from the views we have today. They thought that if life was hard, that was how God had made it and how he wanted it to stay. Everyone had their place. Men were better than women, and children had hard lives. Some people would always be rich, others would always be poor, but in heaven, everyone would be the same.

See for yourself

The Globe Theatre, London

The theatre was one place where both rich and poor could enjoy themselves. Ordinary workers could afford to stand in the area in front of the stage. Only the rich could afford a seat in the best balconies. This is a reconstruction of the Globe Theatre, London. In the original theatre, plays were performed by the Lord Chamberlain's Men, a band of actors that included William Shakespeare. Shakespeare wrote plays for these actors. Shakespeare's plays are still performed at the Globe Theatre today.

Education

Schools were mainly for rich children. They were grammar schools, founded by wealthy **merchants**. Most pupils were boys; few girls were educated. The school day lasted from 7 a.m. to 5 p.m. The most important subjects were Latin and religion. Pupils wrote with a quill pen, made from a feather with a sharpened point.

Food and drink

Most rich Tudors ate well. The main part of each meal was meat. By law, everyone had to eat fish, not meat, on Fridays and during Lent. Until the 1580s, vegetables and fruit were less popular. By 1600, there were many more vegetable and fruit gardens, and new varieties were available, but only for the rich. Most Tudor **households** also brewed their own beer. The poor, of course, were often short of food.

Young children learned to read from a 'horn book' like this one, either in a nursery or at home. On a sheet of transparent horn were written the alphabet and the Lord's Prayer, which children had to learn by heart.

Exploring further

Use the Heinemann Explore CD-ROM or visit the website to find out more about:

- the *Homily of Obedience*, which shows how the Tudors believed God had ordered the world. Look in 'Written Sources'.

- the Globe Theatre. Start by looking in 'Media Bank'.

How did knowledge of the world change during the Tudor period?

During Tudor times, explorers found new lands and met the people who lived in them. Before then, people in Britain did not know that North and South America lay across the Atlantic Ocean. The Tudors also tried to work out the positions of the **continents**.

A wider world

In Tudor times, sailors from lots of different countries went on voyages of exploration. In 1492, Christopher Columbus sailed across the Atlantic Ocean to America. In 1522, Ferdinand Magellan and his expedition became the first people to sail all the way around the world. The world was larger than Europeans thought. Traders were eager to explore the new lands.

John Cabot

In 1497, John Cabot sailed from England westwards in a tiny ship with 18 men. He hoped to find a new route to China. He landed in Newfoundland, Canada (which he thought was Asia), and set up the English flag. He saw no people, but discovered rich fishing grounds. He was disappointed to find no **spices** or gold. Cabot set out again in 1498, this time with five ships. What happened to them is a mystery, as no ships ever returned.

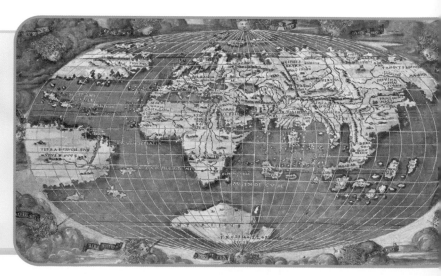

This map of the world was made in about 1508. By then, Columbus had sailed across the Atlantic Ocean to the Americas but, as the map shows, people still thought these were islands, and that you could sail past them to reach China.

Spain and Portugal

Europeans were quick to make the most of the new possibilities. By 1540, Spain had seized Mexico and much of South America. This new world was rich in silver and gold. Portugal controlled the trade routes by sea round Africa to India, China, and Japan. They also went over to South America and set up a large colony in Brazil.

In 1580, King Philip II of Spain also became the king of Portugal. He was now the ruler of a very rich **empire**.

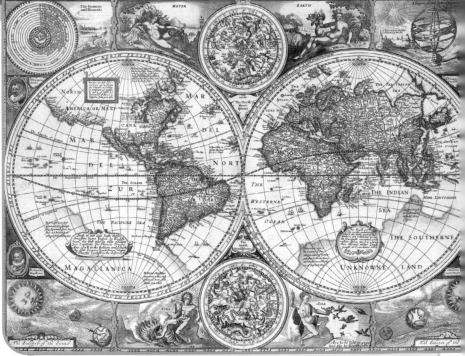

This map of the world was made in 1626, 23 years after the end of Tudor times. It shows that as a result of exploration by several countries, people had a much more accurate understanding of the continents.

Exploring further

Use the Heinemann **Explore** CD-ROM or visit the website to find out more about the routes taken by Tudor explorers, in an animated map. Look in 'Media Bank'.

In 1589, Richard Hakluyt wrote a book about the sea trips of Tudor times. It encouraged other Englishmen to make more voyages overseas. Here he lists many of the places that Englishmen went to in the reign of Elizabeth I:

Which other kings of this land had their banners seen in the Caspian Sea? Which of them ever dealt with the Emperor of Persia, as Her Majesty has done ... ? Whoever saw before her reign an English ambassador at Constantinople [the main city of the mighty Ottoman Turkish Empire]? Who found English consuls and agents at Tripoli in Syria, at Aleppo, at Babylon, at Balsara and, which is more, who ever heard of Englishmen at Goa [in India] before now?

Why did the Tudors explore outside Europe?

Tudor rulers wanted to find new lands and new places to trade. More trade meant more money for England. Some exploration was also to encourage people in new lands to become Christians. Others explored because they were looking for new places to live, where they could practise their religion freely.

Looking for a north-west passage

Some English sailors thought they could get to Asia by sailing around the top of North America. The Tudors called this the north-west passage. Between 1576 and 1578, Martin Frobisher made three trips to find the north-west passage. He got as far as Baffin Island, which is in Canada. He tried to start a **colony** there, but the land was not good for growing crops. From 1585 to 1587, John Davis also tried to find the north-west passage. He did not find it, but he explored Greenland and met the Inuit people.

Martin Frobisher (1535 –1594) died from wounds he received in a battle with the Spanish. In 1585, Frobisher sailed as second-in-command to Sir Francis Drake on an expedition to attack the Spanish West Indies. Then, in 1588 he played a big part in helping to defeat the Spanish **Armada.**

This painting shows three of the greatest Elizabethan seafarers: Thomas Cavendish (1560–1592), Francis Drake (1540–1596) and John Hawkins (1532–1595). Cavendish sailed around the world eight years after Drake. Hawkins was Drake's older cousin. He took slaves from Africa and traded them to the Spanish in the West Indies in return for sugar and gold. He later became a pirate, attacking Spanish treasure ships at sea.

Chancellor sails north-east

In 1553, Richard Chancellor led an expedition to find a north-eastern passage to Asia. He sailed into the White Sea and landed in Russia. A company was set up to deal with the trade between England and Russia. It did very well. During Elizabeth I's reign, trade companies linked England with ports in Venice, North Africa, and the East Indies. By the end of the Tudor age, England was trading with countries all over the world.

English settlers in America

Elizabeth I and her **courtiers** wanted to start up new colonies overseas, in case England became overcrowded. In the 1580s, Sir Walter Raleigh set up a colony on the east coast of North America. He called it Virginia. However, it did not last. In 1607, a new English colony was set up at Jamestown, Virginia.

Exploring further

Use the Heinemann Explore CD-ROM or visit the website to find out more about the Tudor slave trade. Look in 'Media Bank' to see an animation about this.

How did people explore the world in Tudor times?

The Tudors explored the world in ships. During Tudor times, the design of the ships improved, and instruments were developed to help sailors find their way at sea.

New ships

In the 1500s, bigger and faster ships were built in Europe. These new ships could sail across oceans. They were armed with **cannons** and used to fight rivals and conquer weaker peoples. They had three or four masts, with both square and triangular sails. They sailed well in light or strong winds, and were more

This painting shows Tudor shipbuilders at work.

easily steered than older ships. Known as **galleons**, the new ships were good for both trading and fighting.

Helpful instruments

To **navigate**, or find their way when at sea, sailors used a variety of instruments. One important instrument was the astrolabe. The astrolabe worked out where the Sun was. A sailor could then work out how far north or south of the **equator** he was, as well as what time it was.

Life on board ship

The sailors lived in the bow (front) of the ship, while the captain and officers had cabins in the sterncastle, at the rear. Cannons were ranged along the upper decks. The sailors were heavily armed to fight pirates, rival traders, or the people in the new lands they explored.

Life on a ship was very hard. One man who sailed around the world with Ferdinand Magellan wrote, 'We ate crumbs of sea biscuits all full of **weevils** (beetles) ... We drank yellowish water that was foul.' Most sailors did not wash or change their clothes, and were covered in lice. Many became ill with **scurvy** because they were not eating fresh vegetables and fruit.

See for yourself

Golden Hinde Museum, London Docks

The *Golden Hinde* is an exact copy of Sir Francis Drake's Tudor galleon. It was built in 1973 and is completely seaworthy, in fact it, too, has sailed around the world. On board you can see how Tudor sailors lived. There was always a lot of work to be done. The crew would be put into groups called watches. Each watch would work for four hours, then rest for four hours. They did jobs such as mending and putting up the sails, and keeping a lookout for land, storms, or enemy ships.

Why did Drake circumnavigate the world?

Sir Francis Drake was a sailor during Elizabeth I's time. Between 1577 and 1580, he became the first English sea captain to sail around the world.

Exploring the Pacific Ocean

Geographers wanted to know if Asia and America were joined, and if there was a sea channel between the north Atlantic and the north Pacific. They also wanted to know if there was a large southern **continent**, as yet unknown.

Finding new riches

Most seamen were more interested in Spanish gold. Drake was a **privateer** before 1577, robbing Spanish ships and ports and taking their gold and silver back to England and the queen. He became very rich. He had heard about the Pacific Ocean. Now he wanted to sail into and across the Pacific, and onwards round the world, looking for new ways to get other lands and riches. The queen supported his voyage.

This miniature painting of Drake was made soon after he returned from his voyage around the world.

This map shows Sir Frances Drake's voyages around the world.

A December 1577: Drake leaves England with five ships. **B** summer 1578: Drake abandons two of his ships. **C** autumn 1578: two more ships drop out of the voyage. **D** June 1579: Drake lands at Nova Albion. **E** autumn 1579: Drake reaches the Spice Islands. **F** September 1580: Drake lands at Plymouth with spices and treasures.

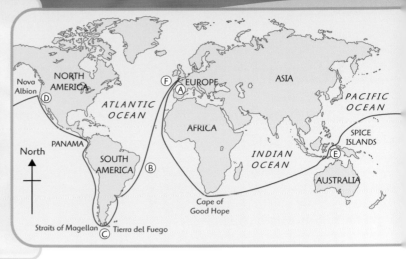

The voyage

Drake was given five ships and about 200 men. Off Africa, he captured several ships, as well as a sailor who knew the coast of Brazil and so would be useful as a **navigator**. Off the west coast of South America, Drake seized a Spanish silver ship and its treasure. He also captured two local seamen who gave him maps to guide him across the Pacific, which no English seaman had ever crossed.

Before he crossed the Pacific, Drake stopped in a place he called Nova Albion, now called California, USA. Here he was safe from the Spanish and could repair his ship. He then crossed the Pacific and reached Indonesia. In 1580, he sailed west across the Indian Ocean and round the tip of Africa. He landed back home in Plymouth on 26 September 1580. The Spanish demanded their silver back, but in England, the 'master thief of the unknown world' was welcomed as a hero. Queen Elizabeth I knighted Drake in 1581. She let him keep £10,000 worth of the treasure, and gave his crew £10,000. She kept £300,000 for herself.

Queen Elizabeth I

Elizabeth I (1533–1603) became Queen of England in 1558. She was the daughter of Henry VIII and Anne Boleyn. Elizabeth never married. She tried to make the Church of England acceptable to both her **Protestant** and her **Catholic** subjects. She also tried to keep England out of the religious wars going on in Europe. However in 1585, England went to war with Catholic Spain. In 1588, the Spanish **Armada** attacked England. The Armada was defeated, but the expensive war with Spain continued. By the time Elizabeth died, she had proved that a woman could rule a country as well as a man.

Why did the Roanoke settlement fail?

English explorers and settlers continued to look for new lands. Spain was still in control of South America, but North America offered more opportunities. Some went looking for gold. Others hoped to start new lives. The first attempts at settlement went badly, but people kept trying.

Raleigh and Roanoke

The English began by trying to set up settlements on the east coast of what is now the USA. **Colonies** here offered adventure, trade, and freedom for people seeking to escape poverty or religious persecution at home. Sir Walter Raleigh was a soldier and **courtier**, and a favourite of Elizabeth I. He paid for two ships to sail to Roanoke Island, now in modern North Carolina. The sailors found grapes growing. The local people, who they called **Indians**, were friendly. So, in 1585, 300 colonists and 300 soldiers landed there.

Failure

The settlers found they could not grow enough crops to survive. Also, the soldiers quarrelled with the Indians. When Francis Drake while on a raiding voyage, arrived looking for supplies, the colonists sailed home with him.

After the failure of the Roanoke settlement, Raleigh went to South America in search of the mythical gold mines of El Dorado, but that also failed.

A second attempt

In the summer of 1587, Raleigh sent a second expedition to Roanoke. A group of 84 men, 17 women, and 11 children set up a colony there. A month later, their leader, John White, sailed to England for supplies. It took him three years to get money and supplies for the colony, because England was at war with Spain. By the time he returned to Roanoke, the colonists had disappeared. No one is sure what happened to them.

This is what White wrote about finding the empty colony. He thought the settlers had gone to live somewhere else:

We fired our guns near the shore and blew our trumpets and sang English songs, but we heard no answer ... The houses had been taken down ... Many of my things lay about the place spoiled and broken ... I was sad to lose my things, but very happy that the people must be safe.

Learning a lesson

The English had learned that settlers must be able to grow their own food and make the things they needed. In 1607, a new English colony was founded at Jamestown, Virginia, USA. Its leader was John Smith. The colonists bought **corn** from the Indians and learned to grow **tobacco**, which they sold to England. These settlers had come to stay.

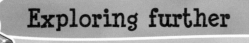

Exploring further

Use the Heinemann Explore website or CD-ROM to find out more about settling and living in the New World in the Activity 'Exploring the New World'.

What were the effects of the English settlement on the people living in America?

Tudors called the people who lived in America **Indians**. This was because the first explorers thought they had landed in the 'Indies', or Asia. At first the Indians did not mind the settlers, but soon there were fights between the two groups.

Attitude problems

Many settlers did not think the Indians were bad. They just thought they were not as good at things as themselves. They thought that the Indians should copy their ways. The Indians disagreed.

John White, the Governor of the Roanoke **colony**, made drawings of the Indians, such as this one of a man with a bow.

Sailors and settlers would often write about the Indians to their families back in England. In 1588, an explorer called Thomas Hariot wrote this:

They are a people clothed with loose mantles [capes] made of deerskins, and aprons ... round about their middles; all else naked ... The only weapons they have are bows made of witch hazel, and arrows of reeds, and also flat-edged truncheons [blocks] of wood about a yard [a metre] long.

Their towns are small, and near the sea coast ... the greatest that we have seen have been of only 30 houses ... Compared to us they are a poor people, and they lack skill ... Yet they seem very clever ... they show great ability in the things that they do ... And when they find that our ways are so much more perfect than theirs, they will [want] our friendship and love, and try hard to please and obey us.

After coming back from Roanoke, a settler called Ralph Lane wrote:

*The savages [Indians] made us a weir [trap] for fish and sowed **corn** for us ... They and other Indians did plot against us. They would not trade, and set fire to the houses around the fort. Then we heard that there would be another attack, so I went to seize their canoes, so they could not get at us, but fighting broke out, and their chief was killed.*

The towne of Pomeiock and true forme of their howses, couered and enclosed some wth matts, and some wth barcks of trees. All compaßed abowt wth smale poles stock thick together in stedd of a wall.

This painting of an Indian village in America was made by an Englishman in 1585. There were plenty of surprises in store for the newcomers. They had never seen turkeys, **tobacco**, or potatoes before.

What impact has Tudor exploration had on our lives today?

The Tudor exploration of the world had some good and some less good long-term effects.

Learning about the world

Tudor exploration taught geographers and other people more about the world. This made it possible for others to explore further, over the next centuries. More accurate maps of the world were drawn, and people learned more about peoples in foreign lands.

This is a page from a book of sea charts called *Mariner's Mirrour*. It was published in England in 1588, and included information learned by Tudor explorers. It was widely used by British seamen **navigating** the world for the next 100 years.

Trade

England was quite a small country compared with France and Spain. However, by the end of the Tudor age, England had a powerful navy and was beginning to build a trading **empire** across the world.

Trade brought new products to England. It still does today. In Tudor times, new products from America included potatoes, turkey, **maize,** and **tobacco**.

Without Tudor exploration we wouldn't enjoy many of the foods that we eat today.

Empire building

The English began more settlements in North America. The French and Spanish also had settlements there, but theirs were only outposts for traders, soldiers, and priests. The English were the first Europeans to settle there in large numbers.

Over the next 300 years, the British settled in other countries where they traded. Gradually they began to rule these countries too, forming an empire. By 1920, it was the biggest empire in the world. Today, almost all the countries that were in this empire, from Canada and South Africa to India and Australia, rule over themselves again.

Exploring further

Use the Heinemann Explore CD-ROM or visit the website to find out more about exploration in Tudor times. Look in 'Digging Deeper, Tudor Explorers.'

Timeline

1485	Henry Tudor fights Richard III to win the Battle of Bosworth and becomes King Henry VII, the first Tudor King
1491	Henry VIII is born
1492	Christopher Columbus sails across the Atlantic Ocean and reaches America
1509	Henry VIII becomes King of England and marries Katharine of Aragon
1516	Mary is born
1517	Martin Luther starts the **Protestant Reformation** in Germany
1522	Ferdinand Magellan of Spain is the first person to sail right around the world
1529-1539	English Reformation, including the closing of the **monasteries**. The Church of England is established.
1533	Henry divorces Katharine of Aragon and marries Anne Boleyn. Elizabeth is born.
1536	Anne Boleyn is **beheaded**. Henry marries Jane Seymour.
1537	Edward is born. Jane Seymour dies.
1540	Henry marries and divorces Anne of Cleves and marries Catherine Howard.
1543	Henry marries Catherine Parr.
1547	Henry VIII dies and his son becomes Edward VI.
1553	Edward VI dies. The **Catholic** Mary becomes Queen of England. Richard Chancellor leads an expedition to find a north-eastern passage to Asia.
1554-1558	England and Wales become Catholic again
1558	On the death of Mary, Elizabeth I becomes Queen of England
1562	John Hawkins becomes the first English slave trader
1564	William Shakespeare is born
1576-1578	Martin Frobisher makes three voyages to find a north-western passage to Asia
1580	Francis Drake completes his circumnavigation of the world
1585 and 1587	Sir Walter Raleigh tries to establish a settlement at Roanoke in America
1588	The Spanish Armada is defeated
1600	The East India Company is founded for trade
1603	Elizabeth I dies and the Tudor dynasty ends. The new king is James I, who was already King James VI of Scotland. He is the first British monarch of the Stuart dynasty.

See for yourself *this order is thematic, to reflect the book's contents*

Hampton Court Palace, London
Henry VIII's royal palace on the banks of the River Thames is full of evidence from Tudor times.

Hever Castle, Kent
This was the childhood home of Anne Boleyn, and was later given by Henry VIII to Anne of Cleves. It contains Tudor portaits, furniture, and tapestries.

Sudeley Castle, Gloucestershire
This was the home of Catherine Parr before and after her marriage to Henry VIII. As well as Tudor rooms, there is an exhibition of reproduction costumes worn by Henry and his wives.

National Portrait Gallery, London
The gallery has portraits of Henry VIII and his wives, as well as many other leading Tudor figures.

Speke Hall, Liverpool
One of the finest half-timbered mansions to have survived in England. In Tudor times it was home to the Norris family. Inside, it has been considerably altered over the centuries.

Bramall Hall, Stockport
This is another fine half-timbered house, the home of the Davenport family.

Tudor Old Hall, Tatton Park, Knutsford
The house was built in about 1520 by Sir Thomas Egerton, who became Lord Chancellor. Several rooms from the period survive.

Kentwell Hall, Long Melford, Suffolk
This lovely redbrick Tudor mansion was built between 1500 and 1550 as the home of the Clopton family. It is surrounded by a moat. The house has many Tudor features, and hosts Tudor re-creation events.

Tudor Merchant's House, Tenby, Pembrokeshire
This Tudor house has remains of early frescoes, and is furnished to re-create family life from the Tudor period onwards.

The Globe Theatre, London
The theatre in which Shakespeare and his acting group performed their plays has been accurately reconstructed close to its original site in Bankside, London.

Shakespeare's Birthplace, Stratford-upon-Avon
The house in which Shakespeare was born and grew up has been beautifully restored and offers an excellent insight into the lives of a Tudor gentleman's family. In the nearby village of Shottery is Anne Hathaway's cottage. This farmhouse was the home of Shakespeare's wife before they married.

Pendennis Castle, Falmouth, Cornwall
This fort was one of a series built in the 1540s by Henry VIII to strengthen the coastal defences against invasion from Spain and France. Today, as well as the castle, there is a museum and a discovery centre to visit.

Burghley House, Stamford, Lincolnshire
This is one of the largest and grandest houses of the time of Elizabeth I. It was built by William Cecil, Lord Burghley, who was Lord High Treasurer under Elizabeth I from 1555 to 1587.

Hardwick Hall, Chesterfield, Derbyshire
One of Britain's greatest and most complete Elizabethan houses, home of 'Bess of Hardwick'. The house is remarkable for being almost unchanged since Bess lived there, giving a rare insight into the formality of court life in the Elizabethan age. There are collections of 16th-century embroideries, tapestries, furniture, and portraits.

The Mary Rose, Portsmouth
The *Mary Rose* is the only 16th century warship on display anywhere in the world. It was built between 1509 and 1511, and was a favourite of Henry VIII's. The ship sank in 1545 off the coast of Portsmouth, and was discovered and finally brought to the surface in 1982. As well as the remains of the ship, there is a large exhibition of objects found on board and a re-creation of the life of a Tudor sailor.

Golden Hinde Museum, London docks
The museum is an accurate reconstruction of the ship in which Francis Drake sailed round the world.

Buckland Abbey, Devon
This former monastery was sold by Henry VIII to Sir Richard Grenville, who built his new house around the abbey church. Grenville sold it to Sir Francis Drake after his circumnavigation, and it remained the Drake ancestral home until the 1940s. It has a 16th-century great hall, and an exhibition of seafaring items from the time of Drake.

Glossary

alliance friendship with another group or country

alms money given to the poor for food and clothes

armada fleet of ships

behead method of killing a person by cutting off their head with a sword or an axe

cannon large gun

cardinal important official in the Catholic church

Catholic Catholics are Christians who recognize the pope in Rome as head of the church

citizen member of a country or empire

coat of arms design on a shield that represents a family

colony community of settlers in a new country

condemn strongly disapprove of something

continent one of the main masses of land in the world. There are seven continents: Europe, Asia, Africa, Oceania, North America, South America, and Antarctica.

corn food plant unknown in Europe before the exploration of America

court king or queen's home and the people who live with and work for the monarch. Also a place where law trials are held.

courtier person who attends the royal court as a companion or adviser to the monarch

empire group of countries controlled by another country

equator imaginary line around the middle of the Earth

galleon large vessel with three or four masts used as a merchant ship or warship

govern run a country

government the people who run a country

half-timbered method of building a house used in Tudor times. The walls are made of a timber frame with plaster in between the timbers.

harpsichord musical instrument with a keyboard, like a piano

heir someone to be the next ruler

household people who live with and work for the owner of a house

Indian Columbus called the people of America Indians, believing he was in the 'Indies' (Asia)

inventory list of possessions

lute musical instrument with strings

joust competition between armed knights on horseback

Justice of the Peace local government official, first set up in Elizabethan times

lady-in-waiting female helper who looks after a queen or princess

maize tall kind of corn, with large seeds

merchant person who makes their living by buying and selling things, either in their own country or abroad

minister member of the government who works for and advises the monarch

monarch king or queen

monastery religious place where monks live together

navigate find the way, especially at sea

Parliament the House of Commons and the House of Lords, which meet in London to advise the ruler and make laws. In Tudor times, members of the House of Commons were elected by wealthy voters; the House of Lords was made up of noblemen and important church officials.

parlour living room

pedlar person who travelled around selling things

Poor Laws laws made by Parliament to try to force poor people into work, to stop people being vagrants

privateer pirate with a government licence to attack another country's ships

Protestant member of one of the new Christian churches set up in the 1500s to replace the Catholic church

real tennis a type of tennis played on a court with walls surrounding it

Reformation the setting up of Protestant churches in Europe (including England) as a protest against certain wrongs in the Catholic Church

retailer people who run shops or sell things

scholar person who studies a subject and knows a lot about it

scurvy disease that is caused by not eating enough fresh fruit and vegetables

slum very run-down area

spices pepper, cinnamon, cloves, etc. which came from East Asia and were used by rich people to season their food

tapestry heavy sheet of cloth woven with pictures or patterns for hanging on the wall

tobacco plant of which dried leaves were smoked in pipes by American Indians. Pipe smoking became popular in Europe.

vagrant person with no home and often no job, who wandered from place to place. Some vagrants turned to crime to survive.

will the written wishes of a person about how his or her property is to be shared among people after he or she dies

Index